VIKING
FACEBOOK MARKETING

Viking Facebook Marketing Page

Chapter 1:

Intro to Facebook Marketing

Why Market on Facebook?

One could argue that there has truly never been anything like Facebook. The undeniable king of social networks took the web by storm several years ago and has since become a household name. Almost everyone has a Facebook account (and about 3/4 of all U.S. adults check it regularly). There is simply no other platform so consistently and universally used all around the globe.

For many businesses and organizations, their Facebook presence has replaced their actual website (at least in importance) because people are more likely to interact and receive updates there. Is there a blackout in your city or an emergency in your local area? There's a good chance the power company or news agencies will be posting updates on Facebook more quickly and consistently than their own websites. Why? Because *that's* where everybody is. And you *need* to be where your audience is.

Facebook has done an excellent job of developing an environment where people stay inside the platform. Although links to the outside are easy to create, it's now just as easy and perhaps more beneficial to keep things *inside* Facebook. For example, until a couple years ago, most people who wanted to share videos did so by linking to a Youtube video. Today, however, Facebook has made it both quick and easy to upload videos *within* the platform and has even made it the best option by allowing Facebook videos to autoplay as people are scrolling through their newsfeeds, making this option the most beneficial for people doing the sharing and the most pleasing for those doing the consuming. The result? After years of this sort of structuring and positioning, Facebook users now actually feel more comfortable when they remain inside Facebook. People trust and feel safe with the Facebook interface and prefer to consume content *inside* of it. Hence the enormous success of Facebook Native Ads.

The point is, if you want to market your business or brand in the place where your audience spends most of their time and in a context in which they feel most comfortable (hint: you do), then you need to be marketing on Facebook.

More Stats

To fully get the point across, here are some for statistics that'll give you a fuller appreciation of Facebook's size, reach, and importance. Almost 40% of the entire world's online population is on Facebook. Of the remainder who do not use Facebook, half of them live with someone who does. There are currently almost 1.8 billion monthly active users and that's growing by 500,000 new users per day. Almost 1.2 billion daily logins occur and 6 new profiles are created every second. More than 1,000,000 hours of video viewing time takes place on Facebook. Over 250 Billion images have been uploaded, which boils down to about 350,000,000 per day.

And just in case you were wondering about the level of engagement, Facebook users generate 4 million Likes, 510,000 comments, and 293,000 status updates... *per minute*. With a growing and engaged user base like that, it's no wonder more than 40% of marketers report that Facebook is a critical part of their business. The question is, how do you make it work for you?

Paid Vs Organic Marketing

A quick note on paid vs organic Facebook marketing. Ideally, a solid Facebook marketing strategy should include a solid mix of both of these. Organic marketing is an excellent and critical way to provide content and value, keep your audience engaged, gain brand exposure, grow loyal followers, and establish rapport. Paid ads are a great way to boost those efforts as well as to accomplish a variety of "off-facebook" goals such as website visitors, lead generation, and sales. Facebook's masterfully established "native" ad style has made paid ads even more effective than anyone could have imagined.

That said, this guide will focus almost exclusively on organic marketing methods. If you're interested in how to get started with paid Facebook advertising, definitely check out our other guide on that topic. And now, without further ado, let's move on to the first step of any Facebook marketing endeavor: establishing goals.

Chapter 2:
Facebook Marketing Goals

Establishing marketing goals is critical to the success of your Facebook marketing. Countless entrepreneurs and businesses have setup a Facebook presence, made a few posts, and then let it sit untouched for months or even years. This is usually due to a lack or absence of goals. So before you even begin establishing any sort of Facebook presence or strategy, you need to establish clear marketing goals.

Your goals should be specific, measurable, and attainable. They can be long term, short term, or a mix of both. Deadlines and milestones can be helpful as well. "I want to increase my social following" would be an example of a bad goal that will likely result in your marketing efforts petering out after a while because there are no specific milestones. "I want to gain 1,000 likes by Christmas" is an example of a good goal. It's specific, measurable, and certainly attainable. Below are some examples of the various goal categories you might be interested in.

Traffic to Website (Sales, Leads, Content)

Probably one of the most popular goals of Facebook Marketing is to funnel your Facebook traffic back to your own web properties. After all, most businesses don't to business "on" Facebook. You're leveraging Facebook to obtain traffic and convert that Facebook traffic into brand-followers, leads, prospects, and customers. So maybe your goal is to get people to a landing page with a free offer where they can subscribe to your list and become a lead. Maybe they're being sent to a sales page or an eCommerces store. Maybe you just want to do some content marketing and send them to your blog. Whatever the case, the end goal for a lot of businesses will likely be bringing Facebook traffic AWAY from Facebook and over to their own web properties.

Social Following (aka Facebook as Autoresponder)

In this goal category, your aim is to build a large number of followers. This usually means "likes" in the case of a business/brand page or it could mean "friends" if you're focusing on your personal profile. The reason we also refer to this as "Facebook as Autoresponder" is because the main sought-after benefit here is to increase the number of people who will see your posts in their newsfeeds. In this sense, your Facebook posts become similar to sending out email broadcasts via your autoresponder. It should be noted that Facebook has recently adjusted its algorithms in such a way that people tend to see less posts from businesses they've "liked". This means a much smaller percentage of your followers will see your posts in their newsfeeds today than did in the past. Still, if you grow a large enough community, this can still be very beneficial and if your content is engaging enough to get a lot of traction in the form of lies, comments, and shares, you can significantly increase the range of your organic reach into people's newsfeeds.

Passive Presence

Some businesses might have purely passive goals. Simply being present and discoverable inside Facebook is a benefit that has wider appeal and greater utility than you may think. In many cases, a company's Facebook presence might supersede or even totally replace what was once the role of a website. Your business' phone number, address, directions, hours of operation, mission statement and so on can now all be found on a Facebook page and, depending on your audience, that might be where most people seek you out, rather than your website. The ease of posting announcements, updates, photos, and other content without relying on a web developer or having to use a web-building platform also makes Facebook pages an attractive alternative to the traditional website model. This same approach can also be used for events, communities, and brands.

Brand Awareness

Another goal that's less thought about might be spreading brand awareness and recognition. If you're just starting out, there's a good chance your brand might be in need of a jumpstart. If nobody's ever heard of you, a great way to increase recognition is to simply create and share unique, helpful, or entertaining content and get your name, logo, and overall brand identity in front of as many people as possible as many times as possible. If this is your goal, you want to avoid being salesy in the beginning. Ensure you're focused almost entirely on posting helpful, relevant, or entertaining content.

Expand Existing Audiences

If you've already got an audience, your goal might be to make it bigger. This can be done via several social marketing methods. Sharing viral content, either curated or created yourself, can lead to a huge increase in your Facebook audience. Recently, a restaurant in Southern California released a 60 second video with shots of people enjoying their signature menu item, an enormous T-bone steak topped with melted cheese, and it went viral in one day. They had already garnered a respectable audience prior to the video, but after the video, their Facebook audience and engagement skyrocketed (and so did their foot traffic). Although creating your own viral content like that can be great, if you don't have the time or means to do so, you can simply leverage existing content that's already proven itself to be viral by curating/re-sharing it with your own comments or angle added to it. Also, a few humorous images and memes can't hurt either.

Other ways to expand existing audiences can include contests, sweepstakes, and gamification. Assuming your offers/prizes are compelling enough, incentivized sharing can be very effective. Just ensure your methods are permitted by Facebook's Terms of Service.

Enhancing or Repairing Public Relations

Do you want to set your company apart in the public eye? Do you want to associate your brand with feelings of good will and community involvement? Did you accidentally spill a ton of crude oil into the Gulf of Mexico and kill a bunch of fish? If any of these apply to you, then enhancing or repairing public relations could certainly be a good Facebook marketing goal for your business.

You can bet that when a certain major energy giant had an oil spill on it's hands a few years ago and became public enemy number one, they went into PR repair overdrive. They were literally hated by almost everybody and their business could easily have disappeared off the face of the earth. But instead, they handled it masterfully and began pouring millions, if not billions, of dollars into massive PR campaigns to improve their image and highlight their commitment not only to fixing the mess, but to the environment in general. This PR campaign lasted years and you can bet they leveraged social media platforms like Facebook as well.

But it doesn't take a humiliating public catastrophe to make PR enhancement a good idea. This is a goal that any business can engage in. Non-sales related campaigns can include photos or videos that foster positive values and goodwill or even involvement in social movements (be careful not alienate half your prospects) and noble causes. Did your business recently donate to a charity, build a school in a third world country, serve food at a local pantry? These are all things to post about. These don't necessarily need to be about things that your business participated in. They can be content about general things like a heart-warming video about helping the poor or caring for the elderly. Special holidays like Christmas, Thanksgiving, or Mother's Day also present opportunities to leverage emotions, foster goodwill, and enhance your PR.

Market Research

A hugely beneficial goal of Facebook marketing is market research. If you're just starting your business or going down a new path, Facebook can be an excellent place to learn more about your audience and your market. This can be done in a structured way with things like surveys and questionnaires, or in a less structured way by simply engaging with your audience, commenting, asking questions, and so on. Also, lurking or conversing in Facebook groups related to your industry can teach you a ton about what your customers want and who they are. Beyond that, you can monitor your competitors' pages and groups to see what their customers like and what they're complaining about so you can adjust your business accordingly. Creating your own group and engaging within it is another great way to get a constant stream of market/audience data flowing into your business.

Ultimately, your goal should be to come up with one or two ideal customer avatars that you can then base your marketing and product development on.

All of the goals you've learned about in this section require some sort of presence on Facebook. Your Facebook presence can take various forms, and that's what we'll discuss next.

Chapter 3:
Establishing a Presence

In order to reach your audience, gain followers, conduct market research, or accomplish any goals at all, you'll need to establish a presence on Facebook. What sort of presence you create will depend largely on what you hope to accomplish, but the most common first step is usually to create a "page" (often called "fan pages").

Pages

There are several types of pages to create, including "local business/place", "company, organization, or institution", "brand or product", "artist, band, or public figure", "entertainment", and "cause or community".

Pages are different from profiles for a few important reasons. Your "Profile" is traditionally meant for connecting with friends and family and not for business. Your "Page", on the other hand, is geared toward raising brand awareness or promoting your business or cause. With pages you can run paid advertisements, create special offers, analyze data and reports, gain likes/followers, and much more. Pages should be understood as a social avenue for you to build relationships with prospects, customers and clients. Finally, business pages are kept completely separate from your personal profile and bear no public connection to you unless you choose to reveal such a connection.

Building Your Pages

When you first start the page creation process (simply go to facebook.com/pages/create), you'll be prompted to choose one of the page types listed above (artist, public figure, local business, etc). This should be relatively obvious. There is often some disagreement about whether online businesses should choose company/organization or brand/product. In most cases, for online businesses, it's the latter, but it entirely depends. It won't make a huge difference in your page functionality, though, so don't agonize over the decision too much.

Once you've chosen a page type, you'll have a drop down menu where you'll need to choose an industry/category. If you're unsure which category applies best, don't worry – you can change it later. You'll be asked to input a business/product name and hit submit. When you first arrive at your new page, it'll be a little barren, but Facebook has made it very easy to start fleshing it out.

The first thing you'll want to do is write a short description of what your page is about. Facebook only allows 155 characters, so you'll want to not only get the main points in just a couple sentences, but you'll also want to make sure you include any critical keywords that you want to be found for when people do searches. Keep in mind, SEO is still important for Facebook, both for it's internal search as well as for your Facebook page ranking in search engines like Google. Consider using Google's keyword planner tool to determine the best exact keywords to use in your description.

Speaking of being "findable", you'll also want to assign a unique "username" to your page. What this does is create an easy-to-remember unique URL for your page so you don't have a long, impersonal alpha-numeric URL. In the end, you should end up with something along the lines of facebook.com/yourbusinessname, but this will be subject to availability and you may have to use something slightly different from your actual business name if it's already taken (for example, if "TomsTomatoShack" is already taken you might have to stick a "2" at the end or settle for "TomsTomatoes" or something. Don't worry about this too much. It's not like you're choosing an important domain name or trademark. It's purely meant to make it slightly easier to put your page URL on a business card or to make links for your page look more friendly.

Next, you'll want to add your website. From the options on the right-hand side of your page, click "add a website" and enter your main website address (or, depending on your goal, a specific landing page url). After that, it's a good idea to add a second admin to your page. Even if you are the sole owner and employee in your business, you should still do it. This way if your page or profile get's hacked (it happens) or you get locked out of your profile, you'll at least have someone else who can try to access the page and do what needs to be done. This is a security precaution, so it doesn't matter who it is and they don't literally need to ever be an actual admin. Heck, this could be your grandma if you want. After that, you'll want to "like" your own page so you'll now be following it via your personal profile and you'll want to make sure you turn on notifications.

Now you'll want to start visually completing your page. First, you'll want to add a square profile image. This can be an image of you or of your logo, or whatever you want people to see associated with your brand. In addition to being visible on your page, this will also be the "avatar" image that accompanies your comments and activity on Facebook when you're posting/commenting as your business. Once that's done, you'll want to add a horizontal cover image. If you don't have a horizontal image to use for your cover, you can either create one for yourself via a tool like Canva or you can pay someone on Fiverr to make it for you.

Next, go to edit your "page info" to adjust your page details. Here you can add categories, descriptions, contact info, location, legal disclaimers, and so on. Then, go to "see all information" and see if there's anything else you want to add such as awards, privacy policy, and so on.

Finally, you'll want to add a call-to-action button to the top of your page. This CTA button can be for booking services, contacting you, purchasing or shopping, downloading something, or even a generic "learn more". After choosing one of these categories, you'll have a choice of more specific CTA wordings to select from.

Once your page is ready and looking the way you want it, you'll have an opportunity to start inviting friends to like the page or to start posting content to the page timeline.

Groups (private/public)

One option for establishing a presence on Facebook is to create a Group. A Facebook group can be either public or private. These groups can be an excellent way to interact with your audience, share content, encourage them to interact with each other, and even start building a "tribe" mentality among your followers. Although groups can eventually take on a life of their own once you've got enough members in there conversing, posting, and asking/answering questions, early on it will be important for you to have a content posting routine to keep things fresh and moving. It may also be a good idea to appoint a moderator/admin to handle things on the inside. Be prepared: groups can easily turn into a second customer support channel and can also be a place where people think it's okay to dump their complaints or criticisms of your brand. Be sure to keep an eye on things in there, try to foster a "positive vibes" environment, have yourself or moderators on hand to delete/censor any comments that might harm your brand, and make it clear to members whether or not it's okay to handle customer service stuff in the group (it's totally up to you and, in fact, handling customer service in groups is becoming a bit of a trend lately). If you choose to make your group a "no customer support" zone, just ensure you get that message across kindly and gently and use patience when reminding individual members about it. Remember, your whole tribe can see your and will judge you on how you treat members.

Creating a Group

To create a group, go to your Groups page and click the green "Create Group" button. You'll first need to name your group. This can be your business name or a spinoff of your business name. For example, if your group is centered around providing special training or advice on using a product, you might call it your product name plus the word "masters", "experts" or "ninjas" at the end of it. Each group needs to start out with at least one members so you can either add several members right there from the beginning or you can just add yourself for the time being and move on. The final selection is your group's privacy status: closed, public, or secret (secret means it's not even searchable or discoverable). You can change this setting later. After you hit submit, you'll need to choose an Icon for your group. Just pick whatever seems most relevant.

Once your group is created, you can start fleshing it out by adding a cover photo and description. The same guidance for business Page descriptions above applies here more or less. Keep it short, clear, and include important keywords. As for the cover photo, make it horizontal and consider using Canva to create your image or hiring someone on Fiverr to make a nice image.

Personal Profile

The final type of presence to have on Facebook is your personal profile. Although it's true Facebook has terms that prohibit using your personal profile for explicit business purposes, to a certain extent. However, that does not prevent you from leveraging your personal profile in exactly the way social profiles were meant to be used: networking. Make it clear what it is you do and what services you provide. Make yourself findable via search, join relevant groups, contribute to discussions, introduce yourself and rub elbows as much as possible. In this sense, your personal profile can be an incredible resource for marketing and potentially even more powerful than your business page.

So, once you've established the sort of presence you've determined you need, you'll want to start posting content. After all, that's what this whole endeavor has been about. And it's what we'll cover in the next chapter.

Chapter 4:
Content Strategy

Now that you've got your presence established, it's time to start cranking out some quality organic marketing content. Let's look at some of the types of content you can create, curate, and leverage in your Facebook marketing.

Basic Posts

So much emphasis has been placed on visual media like photos, memes, and videos in recent years that many people have forgotten the power of good old-fashioned text. A basic textual post can accomplish a lot and, in fact, can actually stand out a lot today in people's newsfeeds that are often filled with non-stop cliché viral images and videos. A standard textual post can be an excellent pattern interrupt in these cases. A textual post, whether it be from your personal profile, a business page, or a group, can be about anything you want. It might be a piece of content in and of itself, like an informative blog post. It could be a link back to some other content elsewhere such as your blog or website or your Youtube channel. Other great ideas for content are questions, stories, and jokes. These can be great for boosting engagement and getting conversations started.

A newer feature worth mentioning is the ability to make your textual posts appear as bold text on a large colored background. This is an awesome attention-grabbing feature that's definitely worth trying for short messages (there's only room for 2 or 3 sentences). Finally, a poll is a great way to boost engagement in your textual posts as well. Asking questions is already something that boosts engagement and people love voting on things, so naturally when you pair the two together you're likely to get some great social traction. HINT: For polls, always say something like "tell us 'why' in the comments below" so people can talk about their opinions and get some conversations and extra engagement going.

Image Posts and Memes

It's been almost a decade, and we're STILL seeing images Boromir from Lord of the Rings looking at us in our newsfeeds and telling us about how "One does not simply… [insert funny variable here]". Why? Because it gets people's attention, gets your point across, and usually still results in a few likes, shares, or comments. Whether it's Sean Bean saying "One does not simply run Facebook ads without a using a tracking pixel" or the Dos Equis guy sipping on a beer and saying "I don't usually try to lose 5 pounds in one week, but when I do, I use High Intensity Interval Training", the fact is memes work in almost any niche. In fact, it's precisely their goofy and ironic application to unexpected niches that causes them to be so funny and get a rise out of people. So, it's settled, if you can find a few minutes per week to make a funny meme for your niche, it's definitely worth your time.

Other images can be beneficial as well. If you're working an "authority" angle, try posting images of you on stage at events.

If you're promoting a free report or free digital offer, you can use an image of the eCover itself or even a generic stock image Adobe Stock. Make sure the images are relevant to your offer and audience. So, if you're targeting restaurant owners, a smiling business owner standing outside of their restaurant might work. If you're doing a weight loss product, a stock photo of a woman stretching or a man running might be the ticket. If you're selling physical products, use an image of the product itself or of a person using the product. And remember, these are organic posts, not paid ads, so you're not bound by some of Facebook's restrictions like the "text to image" space ratio and so on (although there are still some ToS that apply to all content, so be sure to familiarize yourself with those).

Videos

Video. The uncontested king of engaging content. This still hasn't changed. In fact, if anything, it's becoming even more of a norm than ever. If you're not using videos in your Facebook marketing, you're missing out big time. While it used to be common to use YouTube for hosting your videos and simply embed/link to them on Facebook, Facebook has since then started to beef up their own video hosting functionality. Today, Facebook is giving YouTube a run for it's money and many people are now beginning to lean toward using Facebook as their primary video sharing venue. This is beneficial not only to Facebook, but also to marketers because Facebook has made its videos super engaging by making them autoplay, with no sound, while people are scrolling/swiping past them in their newsfeeds. This results in a ton of views and engagement.

So, video content is a must. But what types of videos whould you incorporate into your marketing? There are several options. Regular vlogs, talking head videos, selfie videos, screen capture videos, instructions, tutorials, tips & tricks, funny videos, motivational videos, animated explainer videos, short "ad" videos, inspirational videos, slide show videos... the list goes on and on. Anyway you're able to convey content or messages via videos is great. More recently, Facebook has introduced live streaming videos. You can literally host a live video feed or show and even invite others on for split-screen interviews/discussions from just about any device. All of these innovations in Facebook video sharing are helping to propel Facebook further into the video marketing spotlight and it's not a trend that you want to miss out on.

Curated and Repurposed Content

Not all content needs to be created by you or your team from scratch. One very popular form of content marketing is content curation. This means finding existing content from someone else and simply re-sharing it yourself. This can be done simply by using the Share button on Facebook to share other interesting or entertaining posts and add your own comment or commentary.

Another way to curate content is to manually republish it. This can mean copying excerpts from someone's blog, a news article, a book, and so on. Just ensure you always attribute it to the author (e.g. "Here's some great tips from the folks at [blog name]") and try to always put your own comments at the beginning or end and/or ask your audience for their thoughts on it. This is a mutually beneficial form of content marketing because you're spreading the exposure of the other entity's brand name (which they'll appreciate) while also posting content with almost no work required on your part.

Another option for quick content publishing is to repurpose your existing content. Do you have ebooks, reports, or guides of your own? Why not take chapter from one of your ebooks, tweak the beginning and end a bit, and publish it as a Facebook post? Heck, you could turn an ebook or report into a whole series of Facebook posts covering a whole week. Have a blog on your website with interesting articles and posts? Why not post a teaser/excerpt from each blog post (old or new) and a link to the post in question? Same goes for videos, podcasts, interviews, and so on. If you've been online long enough, there's a good chance you'll be able to repurpose a lot of content into Facebook posts.

Boosting Content

Although this guide is about organic content, and not paid ads, it's worth mentioning that you can pay to give a little kickstart to the reach and exposure of your organic content. You can do this by choosing any organic post of yours and clicking the "boost post" button. This will open a new screen where you essentially turn your post into a paid ad for a limited amount of time. You can set a budget, choose an audience, and many of the other settings you'd usually apply to creating a paid ad. This will get your post in front of many eyes that otherwise would not have seen it in their newsfeeds. Be advised: when you use this method, your post technically becomes a Facebook Ad and will then be subject to Facebook Ad guidelines that most organic content is not subject to.

Content Planning

Planning out your Facebook marketing strategy is super important. The last thing you want is for your Facebook presence to turn into one of those where you set up a page, post a few things and then becomes lifeless for months at a time (this happens a lot). When people see this, you instantly lose credibility. That's why its important for you or your team to have a robust content posting schedule and strategy. Ideally, you should be posting almost every day at least. However, this need not always be content designed from scratch. Instead, you can set aside two days of the week that are for original created-from-scratch posts or videos, while all the days in between only require a re-shared post from elsewhere or a quick meme/image. Set aside another day of each week for a video post and maybe another day for a community poll. If you have a regularly updated blog or YouTube channel, you can also simply add a new step to your blog posting or YouTube uploading workflow in which after each post or upload, a link should to the new content should be shared/teased via Facebook. There are a number of ways to easily incorporate daily Facebook posting into your weekly routine. It would also be a good idea to establish a daily or at least weekly routine for you or a team member to go through all your posts and reply/interact with your audience if they commented or asked questions.

Tools, Services, and Help

Maintaining a regular and active Facebook presence can be a little difficult if your business is already busy as it is. If it becomes too overwhelming for you there are several otpions for lightening the load or at least making it easier to manage. Firstly, there are tools like HootSuite and OnlyWire that make social media posting, scheduling, and planning much easier. If you'd like to have your content created for you, there are a handful of paid third-party services out there that will literally create and post content for you on a daily basis. $99 Dollar Social would be one example of this. You'd simply fill out a profile of what type of content you want and what industry/niche you're in and let them take care of the rest.

Finally, it might be worth it to hire a new team member specifically to handle your social media marketing (or delegate the responsibility to an existing team member who has time available to do it). This individual would be in charge of posting, commenting, replying, moderating, and so on.

So, Facebook marketing is clearly an incredibly valuable, and arguably critical part of any online business today. As you've learned in this guide, it can be a lot easier to establish a Facebook marketing strategy and routine than you may have previously thought. But none of it will count for anything if you don't start applying what you've learned right away. To that end, start implementing the steps of the following battle plan today.

Battle Plan

Step 1: Establish your Facebook marketing goals.

Step 2: Determine what type of presence best fits your goals and create it right away.

Step 3: Draft up a plan with your team for daily content posting and delegate the responsibility to one person. (Alternatively, if you're a "lone wolf" consider using the above-mentioned tools or services to lighten the load).

www.ingramcontent.com/pod-product-compliance
Lightning Source LLC
Chambersburg PA
CBRC090851210326
41597CB00011B/167